ROSES IN A SUFFOLK GARDEN

ROSES IN A SUFFOLK GARDEN

Copyright 1990 © Images Publications

First published November 1990

Printed in England by
Payn Essex Limited
Church Street, Sudbury, Suffolk CO10 6BJ
Telephone: 0787 72491

Typeset in Baskerville by
Roda Typographics Limited
29-35 Farringdon Road, London EC1M 3JB
Telephone: 071-430 1272

ISBN 0 948134 24 0 *(Hardback)*
ISBN 0 948134 25 9 *(Softback)*

Cover design: Image Factory, Ipswich, telephone 0473 280012

PUBLISHED BY IMAGES PUBLICATIONS
WOOLPIT SUFFOLK IP30 9RP

"It should be remembered that a Rose garden can never be called gorgeous; the term is quite unfitting. Even in high Rose tide, when fullest of bloom, what is most clearly felt is the lovable charm of Rose beauty, whether of the whole scene, or of some delightful detail or incident or even individual bloom . . . here we do not want the mind disturbed from the beauty and delightfulness of the Rose."

GERTRUDE JEKYLL

Frau Dagmar Hartopp

ROSES
in a Suffolk Garden

By

Josephine Walpole

Illustrated by
Anne Rea, *Dip. A.D.*

AN **IMAGES** PUBLICATION

5

ILLUSTRATIONS BY ANNE REA

Front piece and pencil sketches by the author

ROSES IN A SUFFOLK GARDEN

CONTENTS

ACKNOWLEDGEMENTS

My grateful thanks are due (and not only in respect of this book) to Jack and Peter Harkness for the help and encouragement they always give, also I must acknowledge the debt I owe to Peter Beales, David Austin and all the other sources that have taught me about Roses. Those I consciously remember are acknowledged in the text but always, when over the years one has read a number of books on a subject without ever expecting to write one on that subject, pockets of information float about in the mind and surface when needed even though the source may be forgotten. Mindful of this, I thank any such forgotten source, not only for any help they may have given to this book but for hours of undoubted pleasure derived from reading theirs. Finally may I thank Anne for her illustrations and for being such a wonderful person to work with, the Royal National Rose Society for their support and, of course, the long-suffering publisher — who tends to be forgotten.

FOREWORD

Anybody who writes about roses has a captive readership in me, and I turned to "Roses in a Suffolk Garden" with pleasant feelings of anticipation. The author promptly threw a bucket of cold water upon me by her dismissal of Hybrid Teas as soulless, often scentless and a waste of space. "But they are roses," I protested inwardly; and read on, to be duly captivated.

This book is a love letter from the author to her roses. It was with a deepening sense of intrusion that I entered this private and scented world. A garden is richest where each plant has a little root in one's memories and experiences. In her Suffolk garden, Josephine Walpole cannot take a pace without a rose catching the skirt of her memory, conjuring out of its scented petals visions of Omar Khayyam, Anna Zinkeisen, Fantin-Latour, of other poets and artists, of their poetry and pictures, of what they have meant in her life, may mean in our lives; all expressed by roses.

The rose has been the darling flower of the world through all the history we know, and poor is the rosarian who misses its romantic history. There's no chance of missing it here, for one rose speaks up for the Sun King, others for Napoleon, Richelieu, Versailles, poor Mary of Scotland; and naturally we have the pleasure of reading Josephine the author on Josephine the Empress. Characters pop up from every bush.

This is no history book; each mouthful is given as the rose moved the author's memory, in just the right amount to make us want more. This garden may be in Suffolk, but its owner describes a love affair that can be enjoyed everywhere.

JACK HARKNESS, O.B.E., D.H.M.
Southwold, Suffolk

Author's note: I am sorry Jack thinks I am being hard on the floribundas and hybrid teas. Some are quite beautiful in their own way but in comparative terms bear almost no relation to the old fashioned true roses. Others ARE pretty soulless and scentless, sadly more like waxen images than the real thing.

8

Introduction

For years I had cherished the dream of owning a collection of old shrub roses. I knew exactly which ones I absolutely must have as well as keeping second and third mental lists to be selected from according to available space. It remained a dream, though, for somehow lack of space, time or money or the impermanency of several addresses prevented it from becoming a reality. At the same time, my interest in the subject never diminished and, always, I have managed to cherish a few old favourites accompanied by others I felt I needed for some special reason. Always there has to be a reason — to me beds of soulless, often scentless, modern hybrid teas are nothing but a waste of precious space.

Against my front wall green-eyed **Madame Hardy** (Damask, France 1832) and **Blanc Double de Coubert** (Rugosa, 1892) grow space while the **Austrian Copper Briar** (Rosa foetida bi-colour, pre 1590) struggles bravely in a situation it seems none too keen on. An old Pink China Rose flourishes on my back fence while **Emily Grey** grows rampant, tangling with tall conifers and tying herself round clematis where no one can reach her. But I must have Emily. She was Aunt Barbara's favourite rose and Aunt Barbara symbolises not only my childhood but my first awakening to a lasting love of plants and gardens.

9

Cardinal Hume has a little corner near the back door, a come down from Westminster Cathedral which may explain why, although his growth is quite sturdy, his blooms are not at their best in my garden! I had to have him, though, after Peter (Harkness) described him as the ideal companion to ***Anna Zinkeisen,*** the rose whose birth pangs we shared and in whose many successes* we jointly rejoiced. The real Anna certainly painted a few distinguished clerics and the Cardinal's colour is just right.

Of course the ***Common Moss*** appears in my back garden border — what garden is complete without that heavenly scent — also ***Rosa Mundi,*** the strikingly striped rosa gallica versicolor (12th century) believed to have been named after Henry II's mistress, Fair Rosamund Clifford, who is buried in the Old Nunnery at Godstow, Oxfordshire, and a sixth Anna. But this is all a digression, the real adventure started when it suddenly hit me that I could well afford to cultivate nearly half of my indifferent front lawn and plant shrub roses which, judging by the prolificacy of the five Annas in the grass and two alba maxima by the gateway, would be an almost certain success. Now there are over thirty different shrub (or shrubish) roses bordered by eight examples of the little Suffolk rose interspersed with prostrate conifers.

Josephine Walpole
Woodbridge 1990

*Diploma in the Danish International Rose Trials at Copenhagen, 1982
Trial Ground Certificate in the Royal National Rose Society's International Trials at St. Albans, 1983.
Bronze Medal in the International New Rose Competition at Baden-Baden (Germany), 1984.
Silver Medal in the West Flanders Rosarium Competition at Courtrai (Belgium), 1985.

The Suffolk Connection

Unfortunately the Suffolk Rose itself carries no history being a very recent innovation (1988) as one of the County Series of Perpetual Flowering groundcover roses. Only six were available when I bought my Suffolks but the series is growing without, so far, anything to compare with our own county representative — an adorable little rose. Even the first year it bloomed until nearly Christmas, seemingly impervious to wet or windy weather in spite of its dainty single blooms of bright scarlet, foiled by rich green foliage and bright yellow stamens. Alternating with intense green creeping conifers, it makes an ideal border. Originally I had intended to use Dunwich (a little white cupped rose originally found on Dunwich beach) as well but, when I wanted it, it seemed unobtainable and now I'm glad. Nevertheless, somewhere in the garden, sometime, Dunwich and Seckford must both be introduced for the name's sake.

The really famous rose of Suffolk connection is, of course **Omar Khayyam** and living, as I do, so close to Fitzgerald country it has a special significance. When I was planning my rose garden and deciding to move my existing Omar from back garden to front, a well known horticulturist who shall be nameless said to me: "If you must have that thing for its local significance, keep it out of sight. It has absolutely no merit as

11

a rose." That sort of statement cuts no ice with me and apart from the fact that it has a character and attraction all of its own with little curly pink blooms, quartered with button eyes, flowering in groups of three or four amid small leaf, greyish foliage, it has the two most important factors for me — scent and history. Given either or both of those, I'm not too worried if the pundits complain of lanky growth, and massed in beds in Woodbridge's Elmhurst Park, it is most satisfying!

Edward Fitzgerald was born in 1809 at Bredfield House, just outside Woodbridge, and was educated at Edward VI Grammar School, Bury St. Edmunds, and later at Trinity College, Cambridge, where his illustrious contemporaries included the future Poet Laureate, Alfred Tennyson, and his brother Frederick, James Spedding and W. H. Thompson. Woodbridge people prefer to think of him as one of the eccentric academic "Wits of Woodbridge" — the four close friends Fitzgerald himself, the Rev. George Crabbe, son of the poet, the lawyer and painter, Thomas Churchyard and the Quaker poet, Bernard Barton.

Nationally and internationally, of course, Fitzgerald is immediately identified with the Rubaiyyat of Omar Khayyam and it is generally accepted that his translation of the telling quatrains of the Rubaiyyat is by far the most sensitive and perceptive of the many versions. To quote one American publisher, "...it was Fitzgerald who most perfectly captured the flavour, laughter and lingering beauty of these haunting verses" and, to honour his 74th birthday as part of a lengthy poem, Tennyson wrote:

> *"Who reads your golden Eastern lay,*
> *Than which I know no version done*
> *In English more divinely well."*

Strangely enough Fitgerald's Rubaiyyat attracted little attention at first and seemed destined to the same semi oblivion as such translations from the Spanish as six of Calderon's plays and certain Greek dramas. He published the Rubaiyyat himself in 1859 but sales were virtually non existent until 1861 when Dantë Gabriel Rossetti "discovered" a copy in a junk box and acclaimed it as the masterpiece it is.

While generally regarded as an intellectual pure and simple, Woodbridge folk like to think of him as a sailing man — "Old Fitz" as he came to be known to the seamen and fisherfolk of the Deben and Orwell and of Aldeburgh, Felixstowe and Lowestoft. The rivers and sea that had provided solace when his literary efforts seemed doomed, largely took over his life and in 1860 he moved into a flat on Woodbridge Market Hill, only five minutes walk from his beloved Deben, and in the same year launched his first very own boat, changing it a year later for the Beccles built "Waveney", a smart little craft that gave him pleasure for many years and was greatly respected by local sailors.

Jaunts up the coast to Cromer and Wells and down to Kent and Essex ports soon led to longer periods at sea, away from it all, where he could laze and read and steep himself in the salty atmosphere. Fitz always delegated the actual sailing and, in the early days, employed some seemingly strange characters in his small crew. An eccentric himself, he seemed to have a natural empathy with other quaint individualists, who in return gave him their own breed of loyalty and friendship. Although a vegetarian, Fitz always let his crew ashore at a point where they could have a good hot Sunday dinner, a typically thoughtful gesture no doubt much appreciated and one which tells a great deal about the man himself. Devastated by the death of his old friend, George Crabbe in 1857, he turned still more to the river and sea and, after Thackery's death, still more depressed, he bought his famous schooner, "Scandal," named, he said, after the staple product of Woodbridge!

It would be easy to go on indefinitely recounting the entertaining adventures of Edward Fitzgerald and some of his seafaring associates but this purports to be a book about roses! As Fitzgerald grew older his sailing activities were of necessity diminished; ''Scandal'' was sold in 1871 after his henchman, Tom Newson, left him although for some time he used ''Waveney'' for short, relaxing trips on the river. Tennyson stayed with him in 1876 and they spent some time on the Orwell Steamer, but 1877 saw the end of sailing .... ''so now I content myself with the river side.''

Failing health eventually overtook him, he died in June 1883 and was buried in Boulge churchyard. In memory of his greatest achievement and in appreciation of his legacy, Persian roses grow on his grave. One* was planted by the Omar Khayyam Society in 1896 and, in the 1970's, others were added as a gift from the Iranian Embassy.

> *"Each Morn a thousand Roses brings, you say*
> *Yes, but where leaves the Rose of Yesterday?"*
> *The Rubiayyat*

In historical terms there is little else with such a positive Suffolk connection but, spanning the years, there is not only a Suffolk but a very personal association with **Anna Zinkeisen,** a modern shrub rose from Harkness.

As everyone knows Scottish born Anna Zinkeisen (who divided her time between Chelsea and her cottage in Burgh, near Woodbridge) was a very beautiful and talented painter, best known for her society and other portraits, but although portraits

---

Footnote:
*According to THE GENUS ROSA by Allen Willmott, a hip of the rose from the rose tree planted on the grave of Omar Khayyam in Naishapur was brought to England by a certain Mr Simpson and the seeds from this provided the Omar Khayyam Club's rose.

Omar Khayyam

Anna Zinkeisen

of the famous by the famous will always hit the headlines, Anna's talents were much, much more far reaching. As a war artist she produced some incredible work, not least the gruesome wound drawings now in the collection of the Royal College of Surgeons which, strangely, have a certain beauty all of their own. In the same vein, she illustrated many medical books and journals, the drawings, rightly, having frequently been compared to those of the great Leonardo da Vinci. Anna could find beauty in the most unlikely subjects, "I think the human lung is a thing of beauty — the delicacy of the colours is like a seashell's. Few people realise that when they live in towns their lungs go grey blue, coloured by the chemicals in the air; in the country they are pink. But they are all beautiful." I must admit for myself that one little watercolour drawing of a cerebral tumour reminds me more of a cabbage rose than its actual sinister identity.

It is well known that in 1934 Cunard commissioned Anna and her sister Doris to undertake the important mural decoration on the new liner, the Queen Mary, and that, just before the end of

Suffolk Rose

the war, Anna painted the murals for the sister liner, the Queen Elizabeth, for which she was awarded the high honour of Royal Designer for Industry. In the main staterooms the Bridal Suite was adorned with a peaceful, pastoral and very romantic scene featuring shepherds and shepherdesses — the first person actually to sleep in such an idyllic surrounding was Mr Molotov!

Other famous murals included those covering 23ft. by 9ft. for Barry and Staines Limited depicting the Great Fire of London in 1666, including Charles II on a rearing white horse and Christopher Wren sitting under a tree with old St. Paul's and the burning city in the background. At the Brussels Universal and International Exhibition in 1958 the central feature of the Babcock and Wilcox exhibit was a large mural by Anna portraying steam as the versatile servant of man, producing his electricity, providing power and heating for a number of products and processes that are the very basis of the world's economic development. Two more were to celebrate the 150th anniversary of Blundell, Spence and Company, the paint manufacturers, including the Chairman floating from a balloon, and yet another depicted spinning and scientific experiments through the ages and contained Coventry's Elephant, Lady Godiva's statue and the three spires for the boardroom of Courtaulds of Coventry. In more elegant vein, Anna painted a ceiling mural called "Dawn" for the Morning Room of the Russell-Cotes Art Gallery at Bournemouth and when the Refectory Club off Mayfair's Park Lane discovered an architectural rarity believed to be 14th century with vaulted ceilings supported by delicate columns and pilasters, Anna was commissioned to paint a series of murals in the exquisitely curved wall panels. With subtle gaiety and humour, she captured the medieval atmosphere to perfection turning an almost abandoned cellar into a medieval dining hall.

As well as a varied assortment of sometimes extraordinary

commissions Anna worked on book illustrations, greeting cards and prints, animal portraits, poster designs — everything one can think of but never, ever, lowering the exceptionally high standard she set herself. She was the first person since Flaxman in 1775 to provide original Wedgwood designs and last but never least I come to her wonderful flower paintings which are so much sought after today. Like her portraits, every flower was perfect in every detail, in fact each flower *was* a miniature portrait yet never did they appear stiff and unreal. Anna loved flowers so much, this would have been impossible, particularly those painted in Suffolk in their natural settings as opposed to the more formal arrangements. Her most famous flower painting is, of course, that of H.M. the Queen's Coronation Bouquet which Her Majesty kindly loaned me for the Retrospective Exhibition of Anna's work.

The Lord Chancellor, the Rt. Hon. Viscount Kilmuir opening Anna's Exhibition at the F.B.A. Galleries in 1952 concluded his remarks with the words, "When we look at her work, we say, 'All this and Anna too'." For Anna was not just a beautiful painter, she was a beautiful person — physically beautiful as well as in character and personality. The last time I saw her before her fatal illness in 1976 was at the opening of a family exhibition I had arranged featuring the work of the two Zinkeisen sisters, Anna's daughter Julia and Doris' twin daughters, Janet and Anne Grahame-Johnstone. She was wearing a long, perfectly plain, black velvet dress with her naturally fair hair held at the back with a large, black velvet bow. No one could have believed her to be in her seventies, even a well preserved fifty would have seemed an insult on this occasion for the almost golden aura that surrounded her gave her an ageless, almost spiritual quality. How grateful I am that my last memory of her is one of such almost unearthly radiance for, only a few days later, she lay comatose in intensive care in a London hospital.

As well as being a close friend, I was for some years her portrait agent for East Anglia and knew her so well that when the question of a memorial arose, I was asked by the family to undertake her biography, subsequently published by Royles as a signed Limited Edition. When, two years later, it transpired that the book had made more money than I for one had ever anticipated, as some of the initial expense had been donated, I did not feel justified in accepting it as mine. So one of Julia's most cherished ambitions for her mother was fulfilled and the **Anna Zinkeisen** rose was born, with the very generous help and cooperation of Peter Harkness. Delicate ivory and cream, almost golden at the centre and with a heavenly old musky perfume, **Anna Zinkeisen** is a rare example of total empathy with its namesake.

Another wonderful lady, artist and gardener, who has given a name to my next rose was Gertrude Jekyll whose own rose was introduced in 1986. Because of the name and because it is a lovely rose, I should have wanted it anyway, but the Suffolk connection here is that Antique Collectors' Club, the prestige publishers based in Woodbridge, have reprinted almost all Gertrude Jekyll's wonderful garden books in a series of beautifully produced and illustrated volumes. Having published five of my own books, I know well the care and patience that goes into all their publications and the phenomenal success of the Jekyll books is well deserved.

Although only produced by David Austin in 1986 as an English Rose, **Gertrude Jekyll** has all the characteristics of a really old rose. David Austin has successfully back-crossed two old roses — the English **Wife of Bath** and the old Portland, **Comte de Chambord.** She is a beautifully shaped, strong pink but the real delight for me is the powerful damask fragrance, inherited no doubt from her Portland parent, which is something out of this world.

20

Gertrude Jekyll

Fantin-Latour

Gertrude Jekyll (1843-1932) had hoped to make her career as a painter and as a young girl was given quite considerable training. She had a natural and unerring eye for colour and was beginning to acquire something of a reputation as an artist and craftswoman when she had to reduce and eventually abandon such work on account of extreme and always progressive myopia.

Her other lifelong passion was for flowers and gardens, having been brought up in a lovely country house by parents who were equally obsessed and where she had her own personal garden from the age of five. While still in her teens, Gertrude travelled extensively with garden minded friends collecting plants (and information) wherever she went; she made friends with many well known horticulturists of the day from whom she learnt a great deal and she spent much time with plantsmen in the public gardens and nurseries. In her book, "A Gardener's Testament," she tells how, in the early eighteen eighties, she "became possessed by the fifteen acres in south west Surrey where I have made my home" and describes the many gardens within a garden she created and the many combinations of trees, shrubs and flowers used in numerous original and ingenious ways in such perfect blending of colours, textures and shapes.

It was natural as her sight failed to use her artistic talents to cultivate her gardening passion and to help others as well as herself by journalism, writing books and lecturing about her own experiences in garden planning with special attention to colour schemes and arrangements of plants that were happiest together. To quote — "If the ways of gardening that seem to me the most worthy and that I have tried to give some idea of in my books, are found of use to others, it is because I have never written a line that was not accounted for by actual work and experience."

She talks of her early art training being helpful in "the making of pictures with living plants'' and ''. . . my interest in the devotion to the fine arts has always been one of my keenest joys, and, with it, a love of nature, with all its beauties and wonders. And I am thankful to have been able to cultivate a habit of close observation so that even with my bad eyes I can often detect objects and effects that well sighted people have passed unnoticed.''

Reading Gertrude Jekyll's books is a joy — not only because of the prodigious amount of information and advice so invaluable to amateur gardeners like myself, but because of the infectious enthusiasm with which she writes that could induce, even in a totally non-garden minded reader, a fascination for the beauty of flowers and plants through her unique personal approach to colour and design. I would have given a great deal to have known her but can still rejoice in the wonderful legacy available to us all.

My next two Suffolk connections are much more nebulous but they are two of my favourite roses, especially **Fantin-Latour.** The date and origin of this *centifolia* is somewhat obscure but it appears, no doubt hence its name, in many of the flower paintings of Henri Fantin-Latour, to me one of the greatest flower painters outside the Dutch School.

Fantin-Latour was growing in the garden at Newbourne Hall in Suffolk, the home of the late Stuart Somerville, arguably the finest of our contemporary flower painters who, before the young ones went their separate ways, lived there with his lovely wife, Catherine, and their six children. During the time I spent there, the family was intact and a most delightful family to become almost a part of. I studied flower painting with Stuart Somerville for three years during which time I learnt a great deal, not only about painting but about Stuart's personal philosophies of life that made him the super person he was.

The very first time I went into his studio, I noticed a little painting, unframed, propped up on the window sill, which completely fascinated me; after a few weeks of getting to know Stuart Somerville, I plucked up the courage to ask him, ''That little painting — is it a Fantin-Latour?''

Stuart looked at me rather in surprise.

''I hadn't thought about it like that although I see now what you mean. I paint like that sometimes, particularly if I have a piece of very coarse ground — or did you mean the pink rose?''

I had to admit that I meant the painting (at that time I could not have identified the rose) and felt slightly embarrassed at not having recognised his own work. From then on we called it his ''Fantin-Latour''. I loved that little picture so much that, eventually, I risked asking him how much he would sell it for. He had not actually intended selling it at all but he knew how strongly I felt about it and named a silly figure — silly compared to his usual prices even if I had to scrape the barrel!

Every day I look at that little painting hanging beside my bed, a memory of those happy years as well as a joy to possess. Anyone could be forgiven for, as I did, mistaking it for a Fantin-Latour but, for me, the essential Somerville has long since taken over.

Rugosa Alba

25

Henri Fantin-Latour was an extraordinarily talented painter of flowers, also he had had good training from his strict artist father and at French Art Schools where he was sent at the age of fifteen. He spent a great deal of time in his youth copying and studying in the Louvre in the company of many well known artists so that his young life was spent almost solely in an artistic atmosphere. He came to London in 1859 and stayed with Whistler who was able to provide him with useful English contacts, in fact almost all of the eight hundred floral compositions painted between 1864 and 1896 were sold to English buyers! Thinking about it, what English painter of the time possessed the masterly skill or the magic touch needed to portray in the same manner the ephemeral delicacy and fragility of the flowers, the brilliance and translucence of the petals and the striking colour contrasts giving depth and light without harshness or stridence. Marcel Proust wrote of Fantin-Latour, his contemporary, "The painter looks, and at the same time seems to see deep inside himself and inside his bouquets of flowers." Yet Fantin openly admitted that he painted flowers (and portraits) for money, to provide a living for himself and his family, while he actually preferred painting fanciful, allegorical pictures, often based on myths and legends, often with musical overtones, although, paradoxically, these are his least successful paintings and have no particular appeal today.

There we come to the basic difference between Fantin and Somerville. Stuart Somerville had to make a living for himself and his large family through his painting but the love of his work was paramount. He was passionate about flowers, loving them with something almost akin to adoration. "If you love something enough, you will paint it beautifully," he told me quite early in our work together. "The beauty of the flowers you paint comes through your love for them; if you love them enough and you know how to paint, the rest just happens, every one is a small miracle." That, undoubtedly, is the secret ingredient that gives a Somerville flower painting such glowing radiance, such life and vitality. . .

I first met **Frau Dagmar Hartopp** (or Fru Dagmar Hastrupp) in the early sixties before the municipalities had decided that she was eminently suitable for decorating public places so making her quite a familiar sight. I had been asked to illustrate a book on old roses by a lady horticulturist and she brought me at intervals boxes of assorted specimens obtained, I believe, mainly from that wonderful rosarian, the late Humphrey Brooke of Claydon, near Ipswich. Sadly ill health overtook her before the book had progressed very far; some illustrations I sold, some she kept, some I gave away and three I kept. Two of these were for purely 'technical' reference purposes, the third was **Frau Dagmar Hartopp.**

At that time, I thought I had never seen anything quite so beautiful as those fragile petals, delicate as gossamer and an almost silver pink. My painting (or anyone else's for that matter) could never do justice to that transparent delicacy, paint and paper are in themselves too solid, but I loved her for the challenge she presented as well as for her perfectionist beauty until then unknown to me. As I know now, there are many others who can compete but always she has a special place.

Frau Dagmar's origins are unknown but, today, she is one of the best known rugosas. Distinctive long, deep pink buds open to flaunt those silvery petals and creamy stamens. She has the usual close rugosa foliage and their fresh, characteristic fragrance; most growers make a point of the large autumn hips like mini tomatoes but, to me, the hips are nothing to the sight and smell of those magic blooms.

rosa centifolia

The Albas

"If the curious could be so content, one general description might serve to distinguish the whole stocke or kindred of the Roses, beeing things so well knowne: notwithstanding I thinke it not amisse to say something of each of them severally, in hope to satisfie all."

Gerard, 1633

For want of any better way of deciding in which order to discuss the rest of my roses, I will use the orthodox botanical classification. Not that any of them were chosen for any particular classification, just that I wanted them.

I have always loved white flowers. Even more than my old roses, I love the heavenly scented lilies of the valley, that most seductive of philadelphus, Belle Etoile, Madonna lilies and pheasant eye narcissi. While I know that, contrary as it may sound, all albas are not white, my chosen ones are *alba maxima* and *alba semi plena* plus (although not quite white) the old **Maiden's Blush.** Sheer beauty of sight and smell are surely sufficient reason for my choice.

The *albas* are a very, very old group or roses. They appear to have existed in classical times and were probably brought to Britain by the Romans, while there is ample evidence of their popularity in Europe in the Middle Ages, witness their appearance in so many flower paintings of that period. Their parentage is a little uncertain although it is accepted that one parent is the dog rose of the hedgerows, *rosa canina*. I can certainly testify to that this year, a branch of my own *alba maxima* having sported sprays of dog roses! Some experts insist that the other parent is a damask rose while others favour the *gallica*, but does it really matter? The *albas* are a very special group whatever their ancient lineage.

Gertrude Jekyll writes of the albas —

"Important among old garden roses is *rosa alba*. Though it is allowed to have a botanical name, it is not thought to be a species, but is considered a cross between *canina* and *gallica*. This capital rose is often seen in cottage gardens where it is a great favourite; the double white form is the most frequent but the delicate pick **Maiden's Blush** is a better flower. When once known, the *albas* may be recognised, even out of flower, by the bluish colouring and general look of the broad leafleted leaves. The *albas* as well as others of the garden roses, make admirable standards, their hardiness and strong constitution enabling them to be grown into quite large headed bushes."

I must say Gertrude Jekyll is the only gardener I know of who has grown old roses as round headed standards, they must have involved quite a lot of heavy pruning which, to me, is rather like sacrilege. One of her own stories tells of how her pruning was assisted by Jack, her donkey, who obligingly (?) ate the whole of one side of **Madame Plantier!**

Returning to my own roses, *alba maxima* (which incidentally was given to me by the artist of this book), lacks the fragile beauty of *semi plena* but is still lovely and smells divine and has great historical interest witness its variety of names — **Jacobite Rose, Great Double White, Bonnie Prince Charlie's Rose, Cheshire Rose** and **White Rose of York.** The most

30

romantic of these names is, of course, that of Bonnie Prince Charlie, one of the instances of the rose turning history into legend.

Bonnie Prince Charlie was born in 1720, son of the "Old Pretender," the would be James III who, before the birth of Charles, had made three unsuccessful attempts to regain the Throne lost by his arrogant father, James II, whose insistance on reinstating Catholicism in England led to the revolution of 1688 and his defeat at the Battle of the Boyne in 1689.

The more influential Jacobites (James' supporters) suggested that, should he produce a Stuart heir, things might be different particularly if the child could be brought up as a Protestant. James was to marry the Polish princess, Clementina, then only seventeen, who gave him a son a year later. The Jacobites were overjoyed and, as a great concession, young Charles was provided with a Protestant (as well as a Catholic!) tutor.

He was a beautiful child, strong and athletic if by no means academic, and by the age of seven was proving himself an adept with the crossbow. His thirst for adventure soon asserted itself and, at only thirteen, he insisted on accompanying the Duke of Liria with Don Carlos' Spanish army to the war at Gaeta. When Gaeta surrendered, he followed the triumphant Don Carlos on his return to Naples where he captivated the Italians with his youthful good looks and charming manners.

Charles was hell bent on a military career and, had he not been thwarted, would have joined almost any European army that wanted him. As he grew older his frustration with the inactivity of the Jacobites in support of their Cause increased; eventually, after the defeat of the supportive French fleet at Dunkirk in 1744, he decided to initiate an uprising on his own.

He borrowed money and bought military equipment and ammunition, two Jacobite supporters provided transport, another provided an armed frigate and yet another a man-of-war. He was joined by the "Seven Men of Moidart," elderly but loyal supporters including his ex (Catholic) tutor, Sir Thomas Sheridan, and others with useful contacts. In July 1745, disguised as a divinity student, Charles and his "fleet" left France for Scotland. Sadly the British intercepted and, although eventually their ship was driven away, Charles' warship was so badly damaged that it returned to France with certain of his now reduced following.

In the frigate Charles continued alone through storms and peril until he eventually reached the Hebridean island of Eriskay where he took shelter in a fisherman's hut and sent for the Macdonald of Boisdale, Chief of that territory. Macdonald virtually told him to go home whereupon the Prince replied, "I am home, Sir," adding that "his loyal Highlanders" would support him.

Gradually, despite many warnings and setbacks, Charles accumulated the support he felt he needed and there followed many a bitter battle between the romantic Prince with his loyalists and the warlike opposition. Wherever he went the glamorous Highland Prince attracted more and more adoring followers until, on September 17th, they eventually stormed into Edinburgh. The Prince rode to Holyroodhouse to acknowledge the cheering crowds accepting him as their Prince of Scotland.

Here, after routing his enimies, he held court for six weeks while rallying reinforcements prior to heading for London. The attractive, debonair Prince in Highland regalia captivated the hearts of the Edinburgh ladies and added to his loyal following but, meantime, George II was adding to his English troops. By degrees the Prince and the Jacobites advanced into England first taking Carlisle, then Manchester, giving him great hopes of London. However, the tide turned, the English people were hostile and the small Highland army was no match for the outnumbering forces. Furious and fighting, Charles and his

Mme. Hardy

Boule de Neige

following went into retreat in December albeit inflicting considerable damage on their foes as they went. Back in Scotland, Charles retook Stirling and spirits rose again, but the English followed and in the light of subsequent action, his own chiefs recommended retreat. Back to Inverness they were overtaken and outnumbered by the English and Charles had to flee for his life, hiding where he could, travelling under cover and generally living the life of a fugitive.

It was then that the beautiful and courageous Flora Macdonald came to the rescue. She dressed the Prince as her companion, allegedly an Irish girl called Betty Burke, in quilted petticoat, blue and white gown, bonnet and hooded cloak for their journey together "over the sea to Skye." The story of Bonnie Prince Charlie does not, of course, end there nor that of the lovely Flora. History turns to legend here, though, for it is said that the Rose Flora tucked into his bonnet for luck was the rosa alba maxima.

Personally I agree with David Austin that the true White Rose of York was more likely to have been *semi plena*. One always thinks of it as a single rose although there may be a certain subconscious association with the Tudor Rose emblem. Certainly, in spite of its virgin white delicacy, the hardiness and longevity of *alba maxima* is legendary. It is not uncommon to find it growing apparently in the wild, often in close proximity to an old fashioned bullace or damson tree, indicating that once there was a cottage nearby with the rose growing in the garden. All traces of the cottage vanished long ago without doubt but the *alba* remains, having braved all the elements and destructive mankind for who knows how many years.

"Wandering I found, in my ruinous walk,
By the dialstone aged and green.
A rose of the wilderness left on its stalk
To mark where a garden had been.

Like a brotherless hermit, the last of his race
All wild in the silence of nature, it drew
From each wandering sunbeam a lonely embrace
For the nightshade and thorn had overshadowned the place
Where the flowers of my forefathers grew."

Campbell

Semi plena is, to me, the loveliest of all the albas, now reckoned to number about a dozen, although an old garden book, "The Flower Garden," of 1840 lists forty two varieties! The purity of the petals is unsurpassed, contrasting with the prominent golden anthers, and the smell is very sweet without being at all cloying, undoubtedly why it is one of the two roses cultivated at Kazanlik, Bulgaria, to produce attar of roses. The bush itself is so graceful, too, with the characteristic blue green leaves of the albas, a rose that radiates a feeling of sensual satisfaction.

No rose garden could be complete without **Maiden's Blush,** one of the delicate blush pink *albas* with, again, a wonderful 'old cottage garden' fragrance. Known in fifteenth century France as **Cuisse de Nymphe** and elsewhere as **Incarnata, La Virginale** and **La Séduisante,** all her names are descriptive but **Maiden's Blush,** her English Garden name, is drenched with nostalgia invoking peaceful memories of lazy childhood days. I know I was very, very young when I first experienced the unforgettable sensation of burying my face in a dew laden bloom, almost literally drinking in that heady, all embracing perfume.....

"Any nose
May ravage with impunity a rose."

Robert Browning.

The Bourbons

Alphabetically the Bourbons come next although they are a comparatively modern rose, appearing first in the mid nineteenth century and becoming very popular with the Victorians. The leaves have a more modern appearance than the flowers themselves — perhaps one could say they neatly bridge the gap between old and new.

The Bourbon Rose (*rosa borboniana*) appears to have arisen spontaneously about 1817 on the Île de Bourbon (now Réunion) off the east coast of Africa. The only two forms of rose to have been grown on the island were the Chinese monthly rose, **Old Blush China** or **Parson's Pink,** and the **Autumn Damask,** which were usually planted together as hedges. Like two beautiful people living in such close proximity, they inevitably produced an offspring which was found by a French botanist, one M. Bréon, who sent some of its seed to King Louis Philippe's gardener. The rose grown from this seed was called **Rosier de L'Île de Bourbon,** introduced in France in 1823 and, a few years later, in England. The wide variety and many variations within the Bourbons suggests that a number of other roses took part in the later development and there are many unique and beautiful specimens within the group, one authority suggests something like six hundred!

Knowing my propensity for white flowers, I offer no prizes for guessing that my favourity Bourbon is **Boule de Neige** (France 1881), considered by many growers to be the most perfect white rose, foiled by its strong dark green foliage. Needless to say, its heavy old rose fragrance influenced my choice as much as its, palest blush rather than pure, whiteness but the whole shrub when smothered with those perfect snowy balls created as the petals turn back on themselves has a fulsome, almost breathtaking loveliness.

The bud of **Boule de Neige** is quite extraordinary — no one could imagine that it would burst into such a clean, near white rose, an intriguing twist of grass green and deep burgundy indicates that something in the nature of a freak rose might be on the way. The extreme edges of the outer petals are occasionally tipped with burgundy but, magically, it soon fades away.

La Reine Victoire (France 1872) I chose because she seemed so right for where I wanted her as well as for her personal attraction. A fascinating rose, it is interesting to speculate as to how such a French rose came by such an English name which, oddly enough, seems quite fitting. I rather fancy this has something to do with the shape, deeply cupped, and the queenly satin of the lilac tinged pink petals with warmer overtones. She holds well but, contrary to many roses, the incurving cupped petals turn paler while the outer petals as they back away, turn a slightly stronger pink so that in advanced maturity she becomes a beautiful Victorian porcelain cup and saucer rather than a chalice. Of course, the fragrance I love or she wouldn't be there, silken chalice or no!

Mme. Isaac Pereire (France 1881) has a singularly powerful perfume which decided me on a rose of that colour — a sort of cerise magenta which is not really my favourite pink. In every other respect, Mme. Isaac is perfect for her corner situation,

Souvenir de la Malmaison

La Reine Victoire

dense and tall (although yet to reach the promised seven feet!) and with big quartered blooms, striking from a distance. She appears to have been named after the wife of a prominent French banker though little is known of the lady personally.

My most interesting Bourbon, I have left until last, **Souvenir de la Malmaison,** otherwise **Queen of Beauty.** Even so, it sounds a little out of place historically to discuss it when I have still to come to **Empress Josephine** and **Chapeau de Napoléon!**

The most famous rose garden of all time and certainly that with the greatest variety was the Empress Josephine's garden at the Château de Malmaison. Josephine had fallen in love with Malmaison when the financier, Jacques-Jean le Couteulx, ruined by the Revolution, decided to sell. Napoleon considered the price too high but, characteristically, Josephine arranged the purchase while Napoleon was in Egypt in 1798, borrowing enough money to secure the property. Napoleon eventually raised the balance so Josephine, as always, had her own way.

Both of them became infatuated with Malmaison. Most people know something of the turbulent love story of Napoleon and Josephine, both strong characters determined to be their own person at all costs, but at Malmaison they spent their happiest days, enjoying a rare peace, not only from the long war but from the prickly side of each other. There was togetherness at Malmaison.

Josephine's ruling passion was for botany, flowers and gardens, especially roses, and despite her butterfly nature, she was completely dedicated to her garden and gave it all the care and attention it deserved. She gathered together over two hundred and fifty different varieties of old roses which included a hundred and sixty seven different *gallicas* alone. Despite the war and using the contacts made through her "English garden" she obtained many of her plants from England; it is said that in one year alone she bought roses from England at the cost of £2,600 which must have been a very considerable sum of money in those days. In this as in every other respect, Josephine was noted for her extravagance; when she and Napoleon divorced in 1810, Napoleon made over to her the Château de Malmaison as part of the settlement but she still produced liabilities of 1.2 million francs which Napoleon settled for her, likewise the 3 million francs owing when she died of pneumonia in 1813.

Pierre Joseph Redouté was commissioned by the Empress to paint her collection of roses and for this we have cause to be grateful. His remarkable talent deserved such subject matter as Malmaison provided and, thankfully, many of them have been reproduced and are familiar today. Josephine became even more devoted to her garden after the annulment of her marriage and she used to say with pride, "My garden is now more popular than my salon."

If we have Redouté to thank for his portraits of many of Josephine's roses, we must be grateful also to her for all that she did to encourage rose growing in France through her patronage of the growers and the incentive she gave to research and breeding new roses; for that matter, the same could be said of her influence on certain English breeders. One can only imagine the glories of Malmaison in her time — what a wonderful experience it would have been to see them in "high Rose tide." Sadly, after Josephine's death, the gardens went into decline and by the time Napoleon paid his last visit there after his defeat at Waterloo in 1815, the whole place must have been a heartbreak.

Since then the property has changed hands several times drifting back and forth from state to private ownership; it was not until 1909 and 10 that Jules Graveraux, founder of the Bon Marché stores and an enthusiastic rose grower, collected together one hundred and ninety seven of the varieties known to have been grown by Josephine at Malmaison and again assembled them in the garden there. Much as one likes to think of **Souvenir de la Malmaison** having such a romantic history as being the souvenir Napoleon took of his last visit there, it was not introduced until 1843. It is, however, said that one of the Grand Dukes of Russia actually obtained its seed from Malmaison and had it raised in the Imperial Garden at St. Petersburg. Whatever its real story, it remains a most beautiful rose, ''at its best, the most beautiful of all Bourbons'' (Peter Beales). Its delicate pinky petals open to a perfectly proportioned, quartered shape, sometimes reaching over four inches across, while its delicate perfume is definitely inherited from its damask ancestry. One likes to think that the Empress Josephine would have given it her seal of approval.

Moss Rose

The Centifolias

Reading rose growers' catalogues, or any other plant catalogues for that matter, one tends to get the feeling that the repetition is somewhat overdone. It is NOT — certainly not as far as old roses are concerned and these are our present interest. Along with the catalogue compilers, I am finding that there are just not enough adjectives in the English language greatly to vary the descriptions of these lovely creatures. Different as they are in themselves, almost all are beauty personified (or rosified).

The centifolias almost defy description. *Rosa centifolia*, a must for any collection, is the old fashioned **Cabbage Rose** (also **Queen of Roses, Rose of a Hundred Petals, The Provence Rose, Rose des Peintres**), another favourite in cottage gardens of years gone by and appearing frequently in the elaborate and wonderfully painted flower arrangements of the Dutch and Flemish Masters. It is extremely difficult to date the *centifolia*; reading on the subject produces a variety of theories and I think the plain truth is that we do not really know. One expert claims that it has been growing since the days of Herodotus while Dr C. V. Hurst writing in The Journal of the Royal Horticultural Society maintains:

"For many years most of us have believed that the old

Cabbage Rose of our great grandmothers was the most ancient rose in the world... Modern research has changed all that and will not be denied. It appears now that our *rosa centifolia* did not actually arrive until the 18th century and is therefore the youngest of all our old roses.''

Probably nearer the mark is the theory that it is a complex hybrid rather than a true species and has been made up of, possibly, *r. gallica, r. pheonicia, r. moschala, r. canina and r. damascena.* The *rosa centifolia* as we know it would appear to have originated in Holland and it is said that between 1580 and 1710 the Dutch introduced over two hundred varieties although what varieties they used with the present stock and from whence they came in is unclear. Antoine-Claude Thory on Redoute's ''Les Roses'' alleges that a hundred different varieties were introduced in Holland, which seems somewhat more realistic, but remains an awful lot of essentially similar roses, also, as Peter Beales points out, the *centifolias* have a strong tendency to produce sports, notably the Moss Roses. One of life's (most) beautiful mysteries.....

I once read that it was an insult to *rosa centifolia* to equate it with a cabbage, but why? What is wrong with a beautiful soft pink, silky leaved miniature cabbage which smells divine? They really are cabbage like blooms, their heavy heads hanging down as though overweight for what can become a rather straggly, if gracefully straggly, shrub. One is tempted always to lift the lovely heads and breathe in their heavenly fragrance; like the ***Maiden's Blush,*** they evoke that wonderful nostalgia as though all one's golden, childhood summers are stored away in those magic ''hundred petals.'' So famous is their perfume that more than any other rose they are used commercially for the production of liquid scent and for many years were grown at Mitcham in company with the famous Mitcham Lavender.

Henry Andrews wrote in ''Monograph of the Genus Rósa''

45

(c.1797), ''This is the most fragrant of all the Roses and therefore particularly desirable, for although it cannot be ranked among the rare, it is nevertheless one of the most beautiful. Its sweetness joined to the abundance of its blossom, has rendered it an object of culture, for the purpose of distillation, as it yields a much greater quantity of scented water than any other rose. It is generally denominated the **Cabbage Provence,** from the extreme complexity of its petals, which sometimes adhere so closely together as to prevent entirely their expansion without bursting, a circumstance that frequently occurs in the vegetable from which its specific distinction is derived and which we regard to be unequivocally good as we should every similitude of equally easy reference.''

I have already discussed **Fantin-Latour,** my favourite *centifolia* for various reasons, and mentioned my common moss in the back garden. Next in importance in the collection is **Chapeau de Napoléon,** chosen mainly for its glorious perfume and its little bit of historical nonsense. **Chapeau de Napoléon** (France 1826) appears first to have been discovered growing wild in Switzerland in 1821 and is otherwise known as **Cristata** or **Crested Moss.**

Chapeau de Napoléon

46

Arthur de Sansal

Duchess of Portland
the Scarlet Four Seasons

I much prefer the Napoleon's Hat version, the attribute that makes this rose quite unique. The large calyx characteristic of moss roses in this case is much larger and much more mossy with the formation of "moss" (Bunyard describes it as "an exaggerated development of the sepals") shaped like the cocked hat of the soldiers of the Revolution. Think back to your junior history books and the pictures of Napoleon — always he is wearing this striking cocked hat that looks so much like the buds on the rose that bears his name.

Otherwise the bloom is very similar to *rosa centifolia* except that the pink is a few shades deeper.

My son's name is Robert and considering he is the dearest son in the world, perhaps it is a bit unkind to have chosen **Robert le Diable** as my other centifolia partly as a namesake. As a young schoolboy, maybe there were times when the cap would have fitted well and, after all, nostalgia is part of collecting old roses!

Robert le Diable is an apparently undated rose with a bit of *gallica* in his make up. No doubt he was named after the so called Robert le Diable who became Duke of Normandy in 1028, but that would have been long before this rose was born! He is the most amazing rose in colouring — purply crimson with lilac shadings, marked with grey and, in places, deep purple, the colour proportions naturally varying. He is smaller than most *centifolias* and one is ocasionally aware of a little green eye peeping out and adding to his almost novelty appeal.

"There is one peculiarity possessed by rose-perfume only; while all or most of the others are heady, this gives actual relief from heaviness and discomfort, even from that caused by other perfumes."

Theophrastus

49

The Damasks
....including
The Portland Roses

The damasks, *rosa damascena* and the Portland Roses are so closely related that, especially as I have only one true Portland Rose, I am putting them together. As they are frequently catalogued together by higher authorities than I, I feel fully justified. There is, too, a characteristic damask fragrance shared by all these roses which emphasises the close relationship between *damascena* and the Portland Rose.

The damask roses became popular in England in the Middle Ages when they were used for medicinal as well as decorative purposes. This is borne out by the cognomen of the **Red Damask** (oddly enough *rosa gallica officinalis*), the **Apothecary's Rose** which, incidentally, later became the emblem of the Lancastrians in the Wars of the Roses. In actual fact they are a much, much older rose group which seemed to disappear between the fall of the Roman Empire and the sixteeth century when, according to the botanist Pierandrea Mattholus (1501-1577), they reappeared in Italy. They must have been brought to Britain about the same time for Hakluyt wrote in 1582, "In time of memory many things have been brought in that were not here

50

before, as the Damaske Rose by Docteur Linaker, King Henry the Seventh and King Henrie the Eight's Physician.'' According to Dr Johnson too, ''The learned Linacre who died in 1524, first introduced the Damask Rose from Italy.''

Going back in time, they are said to have been grown by the Persians and brought to England by the Crusaders though this seems questionable in the light of other evidence and especially if, as yet another authority suggests, the rose originally came from Damascus. This is borne out by both Mandeville and Kinglake who in ''Eothen'' describes the profusion of Damask Roses there that ''load the slow air with their damask breath.'' In any event it seems strange that if they had come to England with the twelfth and thirteeth century Crusaders, such an important botanist should, in 1544, have mentioned their recent reappearance in Europe. Like all the old roses, a certain amount of speculation attends their history.

Whatever their background, the damasks as well as having such a distinctive perfume are roses of great charm and elegance. There are two distinct strains — the summer flowering and the Autumn Damask, *rosa damascensa* and *rosa damascensa bifera*. The best known Autumn Damask is the **Quatre Saisons,** the aforementioned parent of the Bourbons, one of the oldest damasks and one represented in my own collection. Long before the birth of the Bourbon rose, according to Dr Hurst it was first discovered on the Greek island of Samos towards the end of the tenth century B.C. and used in the cult of Aphrodite. It is also said to be the Autumn Damask referred to by Virgil in the Georgics, the reasoning being that, at that time, no other rose has the repeat flowering characteristic attributed to his rose. **Quatre Saisons** is one of the loveliest roses, a very clean clear pink in colour yet slightly shaggy in appearance with rather crumpled petals. If this suggests untidiness, it is a very elegant untidiness and the greyish foliage is a prefect foil to a rather unique shade of pink.

The **Omar Khayyam** rose is also a Damask as is **Madame Hardy** climbing up the house. Both have those delicious crumpled petals and characteristic damask scent but otherwise are totally different and individual. **Madame Hardy** was bred by Empress Josephine's head gardener at Malmaison and named after his wife.

I have already mentioned the **White Rose of York** and the r. gallica officinalis, the **Red Rose of Lancaster.** According to legend at the cessation of hostilities the two sides in the Wars of the Roses ''crossed'' their roses and the multicoloured **York and Lancaster** (c. 1550) was the result. An unlikely but pretty story and certainly the rose itself gives that impression, the bush looks most attractive in flower, some blooms almost white, some pinky red nearly all over, but most a mixture within the same bloom. This really is an untidy rose, semi-double and rather irregular, but totally irresistible as far as I am concerned.

The Portland Roses are sometimes referred to as the Portland Damasks which best classifies my **Arthur de Sansal.** One parent of the Portlands was unquestionably **Quatre Saisons,** the other is in some doubt. It is assumed by several authorities that the China Rose is the other parent although Peter Beales maintains that there is no connection with the China Rose, that the other parent is a *gallica* without any doubt. Hurst describes the Portland Rose as a China-Damask-French-hybrid. The Damask is certainly the strongest influence, even to the scent, but there is a definite suggestion of *gallica* somewhere along the line.

The rose appeared in Italy towards the end of the eighteenth century and was brought to England about 1800 by the third Duchess of Portland. It was originally known as the **Scarlet Four Seasons Rose** but later became known as the **Duchess of Portland.** Obviously there are by now many variations but my choice is the Duchess herself who was apparently named by André Dupont, one of Josephine's gardeners, when she

Rosa Mundi
rosa gallica versicolor

Quatre Saisons
rosa damascena bifera

appeared in France from England. She blooms on a neat little shrubby bush, beautifully shaped herself, a rich reddish pink, semi-double with a most distinctive centre and, again, that lovely, lovely Damask fragrance.

I know I have referred many times to the damask perfume but, like any fragrance, it is quite difficult to describe. Let us compare the smell of roses to the smell of fruit; ask someone if he or she likes the smell of fruit and the reply will be, "Which fruit?" Ask any gardener about the smell of roses and the reply will be, "Which roses?" If we think of the majority of roses although, like fruit, very individual, as peaches, strawberries, greengages — the sweet fruits — the damask is the lemon, clean and positive and wonderfully refreshing. But, I repeat, this is but a simile, pure and clean, yes, but nothing really like a lemon!

Back to **Arthur de Sansal** (France 1855), my last rose in this combination group. Arthur is another small shrubby rose, so beautiful that I forgive him his tendency to mildew. Masses of deep crimsonish magenta petals crowd together almost in half a ball with lighter coloured backs to the petals adding to the almost rossettish appearance. The close leaf formation adds to his attraction but unfortunately I cannot find out who he was. One day I shall manage to trace him.

You may break, you may shatter the vase, if you will,
But the scent of the roses will hang round it still.
Thomas Moore (1779-1852)

The Gallicas

"Very old are the woods;
  And the buds that break
Out of the brier's boughs,
  When March winds wake
So old with their beauty are —
  Oh, no man knows
Through what wild centuries
  Roves back the Rose."
                    Walter de la Mare.

The Gallicas (*rosa gallica*) are the oldest roses of all and one could probably say in all truthfulness that every rose that has followed has had a certain element of *gallica* in its parentage. We know that it existed in the time of the twelfth century Median fire worshippers of Persia. It was known to the Greeks and Romans, and Linnaeus maintains that it originated in Roman Gaul, hence the name *gallica*.

In quite early times the Gallicas became relatively highly developed and by 1629, according to the botanist John Parkinson, there were at least ten varieties. By 1800 this is said to have risen to over a thousand varieties but many will by now have been lost and one suspects a certain amount of duplication, also perhaps more than one name given to certain hybrids.

Nevertheless the Gallicas do include some of our loveliest roses, also a considerable number of really old varieties are still alive and well. Incidentally, *rosa gallica* has also been called the **Rose of Provins,** not to be confused with the *centifolia* — **Provence Rose.**

Considering the number of superb different *gallicas* available, it may seem strange that I have only three in my collection when I have even doubled or more on certain very special favourites. Maybe it is — it just so happens that, while there are a number in my mind filling an (at the moment) hypothetical space, there are only those three specials at the top of my first list.

Rosa Mundi (*rosa gallica versicolor*) I have already mentioned and she grows in both my back and front garden. The first one I ever had, now an enormous shrub, was a tiny, hardly more than a cutting, slip bought for pennies at a carboot sale and unidentified until she bloomed. These roses are so prolific and their original colouring so showy, they make a wonderful sight in full bloom, more brilliant than their also multicoloured neighbour, **York and Lancaster.** The date of origin is uncertain but this rose was described by Clusius in 1583 and was certainly familiar by the seventeenth century; it would appear to be a sport of the Red Rose of Lancaster, *rosa gallica officinalis.*

Rosa gallica velutinaeflora has the most magic fragrance which tipped my scales in its favour. Another very old rose, undated, it grows on a small shrub, single flowers with rather mauveish pink, veined petals and very pronounced stamens. No known history, beautiful but not with outstanding beauty — I am simply captivated by that delicious smell!

Cardinal de Richelieu (France 1840) is quite a different proposition, well known for his cardinal's robes of deepest purple satin velvet — I mean his petals. This must be one of the richest roses there is, the mass of purple petals incurving almost to an intensely fragrant ball — incense perhaps?

I would like to think that he added holiness to my collection, but was the original de Richlieu a genuine holy man? I think not. The real Cardinal de Richlieu was chief Minister and alter ego to the French King Louis XIII who, although a brave and courageous man, enjoyed poor health and was of an over sensitive nature for his station. He was happier pursuing his more plebian, recreational hobbies than embroiling himself in European wars and politics, letting de Richlieu, as it were, virtually take over that side of his life. Inevitably de Richlieu became over powerful, seeking to influence the King against those to whom he bore a sometimes unreasoning grudge and reducing the powers of the French Parliament in order to promote the Royal (his?) power. His attempts to turn the King against his Queen (Anne) seem unreasonably interfering and bigoted, particularly when the nation was eagerly hoping that one day a male heir to the French throne would be born and, while he undoubtedly accomplished a great deal for France and made himself indispensable to the King, I do not see him as such an ecclesiastically attractive character as his rose suggests.

I still prefer to imagine the rose as representing a holy prelate rather than a scheming politician — forget the history books. Maybe they have a point though, borne out by the fact that rain, far from being holy water, tends to drain the colour from those wonderful purple vestments!

"A rose does not preach — it simply spreads its fragrance."

Mahatma Ghandhiji

The Others

Expressed like that, it almost puts my remaining roses in a sort of "also ran" category but nothing could be further from the truth. It just happens that there may be only one of a species or type or perhaps just a "one off", but these roses include some of the most interesting and best loved of them all.

If it seems odd to have omitted the *rugosas* as a group, I have of course dealt fully with **Frau Dagmar Hartopp** already. I had intended to include in my collection **Roseraie de l'Hay,** a hybrid rugosa, bought locally and still bearing that label. Sadly it proved to be a case of mistaken indentity and bloomed as *rugosa typica,* perhaps the most common and least interesting *rugosa,* which needs no introduction from me. Hedges everywhere and not infrequently found growing in the wild but still attractive in its own way, especially those very long shapely buds and sweet fragrance.

Roseraie de l'Hay (France 1901) is a splendid rose, large, loose and almost double, opening to a nearly flat dish of huge crimson purple petals. The perfume is different to most *rugosas* too — rather like sugared almonds, to quote Peter Beales. Undoubtedly its name derives from the famous Roseraie de l'Hay established by Jules Gravereaux whom I mentioned earlier concerning the resurrection of the Empress Josephine's rose garden at La Malmaison.

Frühlingsmorgen

In 1892 when he bought an estate at l'Hay, south of Paris and overlooking the River Biéure, he found that the garden already contained around a hundred roses which proved a tremendous inspiration to him and the start of his ruling passion for the Rose. With the help of the nurseryman, Charles Cochet, by 1900 the hundred or so roses had been increased, it is said, thirtyfold and the gardens had been completely redesigned around them. The village itself was later renamed L'Hay-des-Roses because of its famous collection.

All the work he had done at l'Hay had done nothing to curb Graveraux' enthusiasm for rosarian projects and he next turned his attention to the Château de Bagatelle where, with the cooperation of the Conservateur (Jean Ajalbert) and the help of M. Theuriet, an expert in Garden design, he provided and arranged beautiful rose gardens using a duplicate of his own collection. As mentioned before, he re-established to a certain extent the Empress Josephine's garden at Malmaison which had been completely let go after her death; in his way, he has probably done as much service to the world of the Rose as Josephine herself. It seemed strange and rather sad to me that no rose had been named after him as one of its greatest benefactors until I learnt recently that this honour had actually been conferred on his wife.

His own garden still exists under the auspices of the Direction des Parcs, Jardins et Espaces Vertes de la Ville de Paris and is now a truly wonderful monument. Roses from all over the world are represented, laid out and grown in every possible way to illustrate just what can be done to display every species to its maximum advantage and to enhance the magical effect of these beautiful creatures. At one time the garden(s) incorporated a rose museum exemplifying everything one can think of with a rose connection — paintings, engravings, books, embroideries, fabrics, jewellery, everything... Sadly it was burgled by some sick minded criminal and, to my knowledge, the contents have never been recovered.

To return to *rugosas* generally, they are easily identified by their many close leaves, rather bristly and heavily veined, and in most cases, rather striking autumn hips. *Rosa rugosa* was officially "discovered" in Japan circa 1784 although it had been noted there around the tenth century. Despite this, the Chinese like to claim it as a native and it is cultivated widely in China today for commercial rather than decorative purposes; in her book "A Heritage of Roses" Hazel le Rougetel tells how, in a recent conversation with a Chinese rosarian, she learnt that, in China, *rugosa* roses are used as flavouring in all kinds of cakes, sweets, and other delicacies, also in black tea and wine!

However magnificent **Roseraie de l'Hay** and however attached I am to **Frau Dagmar Hartopp,** when it comes down to it my real favourite is the virginal *rugosa alba*; somehow, it is in a class apart from all the coloured rugosas with a pure distinction all of its own.

Frühlingsmorgen — Spring Morning — (Germany 1941) may seem rather a modern shrub for me to have included without any particular reason. The plain fact is that it was given to me by a grower at quite an advanced stage because it would not bloom; it appeared a lovely container shrub and I was feeling around for the label when the offer was made — almost like seeking a good home for a dumb kitten! Obviously it feels happier in my garden because it bloomed for me the first year I had it, a pretty single rose, shaded creamy golden pink with maroon stamens. If not my particular favourite, it can certainly hold its own with its more ancient companions.

Frühlingsmorgen is one of a series of, I believe, about seven introduced by the respected breeder Kordes of Germany, in the forties and early fifties, mainly single roses and with a real attraction and charm of their own if one is collecting modern

Enfant de France

Roger Lambelin

Gertrude Jekyll

shrubs or has just the place for one or another. Certainly I'm not looking my gift horse in the mouth especially as **Cläre Grammerstorf** x **Frühlingsmorgen** is one of three crosses on one side of the parentage of **Anna Zinkeisen!**

Enfant de France (France 1860) is a fascinating rose described by Peter Beales in his catalogue as ''A beautiful rarity'' — enough, of course, to make people like me want to have it!

Its name (parentage unknown) is self explanatory. It is almost the tiniest of the old shrubs with masses of green gold foliage, the leaves veined and edged maroon, the flowers appearing from the centre on short stems rather like pink babies in a leafy cradle. I was about to say the colour is right, too, but such is the vagary of the rose that the blooms on one bush are a real (shaded) baby pink, the other, only a few yards away, is much deeper. All les enfants start as fat, almost egg shaped blooms, large for the size of the shrub, suddenly as they fade quartering rather like a damask. Like all my roses, they have a wonderful perfume, obviously a very exotic baby powder!

Roger Lambelin

Anne's delightful rendering of the Lambelin on page 64 is a perfect image of the tiny
bloom which suddenly appeared long after the others were over. Although scarcely
recognisable as the accepted face of Roger Lambelin, it was such a charming little bloom,
we could not resist. The pencil drawing, although even then a little late in his early season,
perhaps better indicates the dramatic contrast within the petals; in colour and in high season,
the rich burgundy and pure white, sharply defined, gives him something of a rather jolly
Harlequin appearance but which can look rather unreal when painted.

I made the acquaintance of **Roger Lambelin** (France 1890) at about the same time as **Frau Dagmar Hartopp** and in the same connection. He was a brute to paint and at that time, probably for that reason, I didn't like him very much. With hindsight I realise the specimen wasn't wonderful, much more purple than those I have now and flatter. After the project for which these roses were intended had to be abandoned, I happened to show the illustrations I still had to the Leach potter, Dorothy Kemp. Her reaction to my particular bête noir quite amazed me... Although I say it, some were rather nice, but she snatched up my despised Roger announcing in her dogmatic Yorkshire manner, "I MUST have that, I WANT it!" How much would I sell it for she wanted to know, putting me, as I told her, in the predicament of knowing what to charge one's friends. To offer it as a gift would have undervalued it in her eyes.

"Why don't we do an exchange then?" she suggested, "come round to my studio and see what you would like."

I lived quite close to her at the time so we adjourned, bearing Roger, to her studio. I politely picked up one or two small items to be told not to be ridiculous about it, then a cup and saucer caught my eye.

"I like that," I said.

"That's a reject, the handle isn't quite right."
(A great many potters would be quite happy to produce pieces as good as some of D.K.'s "rejects" but never mind....)

"I'll make you some cups if you like that glaze," she added.

"I'd love that," I said, "but don't go mad, just one each or something."

Some weeks passed, then one day she walked in with her large basket — full. "I've brought your coffee set," she announced. "I hope you like it."

I was quite taken aback and protested at such generosity on the grounds that I didn't think that particular painting was worth it, but she would have none of it. "If it hadn't been you wouldn't have got your cups, I hate making cups," she replied with characteristic bluntness, expressing far more than flowery words D.K.'s appreciation.

So my coffee cups and **Roger Lambelin** always remind me of D.K. and the extraordinary thing is, bearing in mind that I can be one of the clumsiest creatures on God's earth, the coffee set, twenty five years later, is still intact. As for Roger, he loves my garden and I find him much more endearing now than all those years ago. I must be amazingly lucky — my poor old ex heathland that refuses to grow a half decent lawn seems home to the old shrub roses. David Austin positively discourages potential buyers of **Roger Lambelin** and Peter Beales draws attention to his tendency to mildew...

Yes, I must be lucky.

Louis XIV, the Sun King, is one of the most colourful characters in the history of France. He came to the throne at the age of four following the death of his somewhat ignoble father, Louis XIII. Needless to say, the boy King was received with great joy by the French people who had begun to despair of there ever being an heir apparent and, when he was paraded through the streets of Paris in regal splendour, enormous crowds who had come from miles around shouted, cheered and waved while the bells rang seemingly in jubilation, admiration and delight. Even at such an early age, he had the confidence and poise that stayed with him all his life and, despite France's tribulations during his early years, was idolised by most of his courtiers and subjects. He was brought up by a retinue of retainers and teachers, one for every subject under the sun, and despite the, necessarily, stricter tendency of his mother, was made to feel, verily, a little King.

Until he came of an age to rule (thirteen years old in those days), his mother, Anne, played the part of Queen Regent with the valued help of her chief Minister, Cardinal Jules Mazarin. These were turbulent years for France, the long war with Spain and the internal strife of repeated civil wars created exciting times for the young King, albeit anxious times for his mother. There were occasions when the Royal family and their court were driven into hiding, times when the high cost of the wars rendered them poorer than many of their subjects.

As well as having the interests of France and the King very much at heart and a tireless worker for their cause, Cardinal Mazarin was a shrewd business man with a finger in many pies. He maintained his own castle at Vincennes in almost palatial splendour with fine furniture and décor and an outstanding collection of valuable paintings. Here Louis was able to retreat when times were hard and indulge his inborn taste for luxury and beauty denied him in Royalty's more impecunious days.

Because of the traumas of war, although officially of age at thirteen, Louis was fifteen before his actual coronation, a splendid affair of great pomp and ceremony during which the young King conducted himself with impeccable composure and aplomb. The French people idolised him and were overjoyed to have a King once more, sworn to supreme loyalty to his country and to the Catholic Church. France was still at war with Spain and Louis joined his army to show that he, as well as his men, could fight for his country. Against the wishes of Mazarin and his mother (and despite the fact that he adored her and they had a devoted mother and son relationship), he did this from time to time, needing to prove his courage and his desire to mingle with his people in their various lives heedless of Mazarin's persuasion that his life was more important to France than fighting for her. There were other soldiers, there was only one King.

When the war with Spain was over and France the victor, Mazarin was instrumental in "arranging" a marriage between Louis and the Infanta of Spain despite the fact that Louis was passionately in love with Mazarin's neice, Marie. Again all the pomp and ceremony so beloved by the French attended the Royal Wedding, eventually assented to by Louis for the good of France. For his ambition above all things was to make France stand supreme in all Europe and to reign over a rich and powerful kingdom as a vital and flamboyant, while caring and hardworking, monarch. His marriage to the Infanta helped cultivate this image but it never destroyed his eye for pretty women and the need to indulge in affairs of the heart with the various mistresses that adorned his reign.

Love of women, of the arts, music and the theatre, of riches, luxury and beautiful things never deflected him from his burning desire to make France the most powerful and glorious country in Europe if not the whole world. He worked tremendously hard, putting in as many hours as were needed to keep affairs of state in good order, control the country's finances and give his people who appeared to admire and respect him, what would today be termed "a good deal." After Mazarin's death he refused to appoint another chief Minister; when asked by courtiers and expectant politicians who would succeed Mazarin, he replied, "Me." Rebuilding France was to be his own personal responsibility, to be accomplished in his way, a way in which he had the confidence of success, of power and glory. "L'Etat c'est moi."

In most people's minds Louis XIV is associated primarily with the magnificent Palace of Versailles. The story of Versailles is legendary, history books and historical novels vying with each other in an attempt adequately to describe the splendour and opulence of the French King's Palace.

Louis XIII had owned a hunting lodge at Versailles which was used by his son on hunting trips to the area with his mistress, Louise de la Vallière; he became so sentimentally attached to the beautiful country round Versailles that he decided to live there for part of the year with Louise. However, the lodge was too small for all the necessary courtiers and themselves so, around 1661, he decided to build on to the property. The late King had also owned the Manor of Versailles and the younger Louis decided to make the two properties the nucleus, not just of a summer residence but a permanent home. When he had first conceived the idea of a country retreat, there were insufficient funds available to carry out the ambitious plans suggested, but the idea stayed with him until, in 1670, the decision was made to move the entire Court to Versailles. Versailles would also become the seat of Government for the Crown and its Ministers, so this magnificent Palace would become the showpiece of all France dwarfing even the Louvre.

For over a decade thousands upon thousands of skilled craftsmen worked away constructing by slow and painstaking degrees the gigantic, incredible Palace of Versailles. Marble appeared to predominate, beautifully patterned floors, marble columns and busts, mirrors everywhere opposite the countless large windows to reflect light and sun. Precious metals and jewels, beautiful carvings, elegant hangings of expensive brocades, velvets and damasks, elaborate and complex glass chandeliers and the most sumptuous furniture graced not only the King's personal suite, that of the Queen and her children, the Royal State apartments and the ornate and splendid chapel but the courtiers' wing and that of the government. The King's own suite was designed to give him (The Sun King) the maximum sunlight reflecting also on the white and gold of the décor while, above all, the enormous grand gallery was resplendent in inlaid marble, large windows and mirrors, richly carved ornaments and a ceiling, three years of work for the famous M. le Brun, comprising thirty paintings of scenes from Louis' reign.

When the King and his court, with over a thousand courtiers and his government officers, moved in in 1682, there were still over thirty thousand workers in the two hundred acres of gardens. In addition to the well known geometrical patterns of flowers beds, there were fountains, copses of ornamental trees, pools, statues — everything, including a mile long canal where the King held boating parties enhanced by brilliant displays including fleets of Venetian gondolas, miniature frigates and brigantines. Louis was immensely proud of his garden even to the extent of producing a book called "Manière de Montrer les Jardins de Versailles," drawing attention to the wonderful symmetry of the whole thing, all those acres of perfect balance of flower beds, woods and water, fountains, lakes and statues. The whole palatial structure, palace and grounds, has been called a great victory of man over nature, to quote St. Simon when considering the high Majesty and (self?) glorification of Lous XIV. "In all things he loved brilliance, splendour, profusion. His taste for these he deemed it politic to adopt as a golden rule with which to imbue his court."

As I said earlier about Edward Fitzgerald, one could go on and on talking (or writing) about Louis XIV but this is a book about roses — there are plenty of books about Louis XIV. In fact, I and others have written full length biographies of most of the characters discussed but, here, I have aimed simply to sketch a brief personality portrait of the person concerned in order to link that personality with his or her namesake rose and to illustrate my own reason for choosing that rose (provided it

Louis XIV

rosa rugosa typica

also had other characteristics I look for), because it identified with someone special or interesting to me. If that sounds crazy, so be it — all the best people are slightly mad!

Louis XIV (France 1859) is a most luxurious rose, truly complementary to its namesake and rich enough to grace Versailles. In the bud, it is the nearest thing to black, a rich red-black with the sheen and texture of satin velvet. Half open the bud is the most perfect shape, the black turning to a warmer black-red but still retaining that velvet quality. The hangings at Versailles, perhaps, or part of the Royal robes... Once open it blows quite quickly, almost as if its extraordinary depth and regal quality was a dream of seventeenth century France from which one wakened to find a half blown, deep red rose. Fantasy, oh fantasy......

Ever since I was cast as Mary, Queen of Scots in a school play and no doubt further influenced by my own Scottish blood, she has been one of my favourite historical characters. Her tragic but romantic and colourful story stirs the imagination of most people with any interest in the past so I cannot pretend to be in any sort of minority, in fact, thanks to her appeal to the historical novelists and a bit of licence here and there, she had almost become a cult figure.

Mary, Queen of Scots was even younger than Louis XIV when she came to the Scottish throne being only a week old when, in 1542, her father, James V died; she was later crowned in Stirling Castle at the age of nine months. At that time the Scots and the English were bitterly at loggerheads and bloody battles were fought, sometimes over what now seem quite trivial issues. Thinking to unite the two countries under English rule, Henry VIII decided that the young Scottish Queen should marry his son, Edward, and a marriage treaty was signed when baby Mary was only a year old.

The Scots, however, under the Regency of Mary of Guise, the French mother of Mary, Queen of Scots, decided that an alliance with France to support them against the English would be more politically expedient. The Scottish Parliament therefore annulled the treaty deciding that, if it could be arranged, a marriage between Mary and the French Dauphin would be a shrewd move. Henry VIII was furious and sent his troops to sack Edinburgh, firing the abbey and Holyrood Palace. Acts of reprisal continued, all out war raged intermittently, and the whole situation became so fraught that when Mary was four years old, she was sent for her protection to France to be brought up by her grandmother, Antoinette of Guise.

King Henri II of France sent the Royal galley for Mary for the French were now firmly on the side of Scotland and giving them practical help. Mary of Guise was heartbroken at parting with her daughter but convinced that it was for the best and indeed, in company with the French princesses as well as her doting grandmother, Mary had a wonderful childhood away from the warring factions in her own country. As well as the French royal children, Mary had the company of those of the Scottish nobility who had accompanied her as companions, so the young court was a lively affair. From time to time they were moved from one royal residence to another to allow for cleaning which, of course, added to the excitement of life for the children. Mary it seems was a most attractive girl, always beautifully dressed and cared for and extremely responsive to the excellent education she was given. She was also a devout Catholic, in fact Henri II described her as the most perfect child he had ever seen.

76

Mary Queen of Scots

Mary met her intended husband when they were six and five respectively and fortunately the two children took to each other at once. When they became engaged in 1558, Mary's sixteenth year, they were still, unusually for such an "arranged" marriage, attracted to each other in spite of the fact that the Dauphin was a weedy child and rather apathetic about most things other than his pretty Scottish bride-to-be.

They were married only a few months later in Notre Dame Cathedral amid splendid ceremonial, wonderful costumes, a sumptuous wedding feast and all kinds of displays and entertainments which lasted for days. Mary made a sparkling Queen-Dauphiness and no doubt revelled in all the attention that was lavished on her by the French court and the amazing life style she was following for a girl of fifteen. A year later, probably as a result of such an extraordinary way of living for a girl of her age, her health began to suffer and a riding accident later in 1559 was sufficient reminder that human frailty can catch up with us all.

Meanwhile war between England and Scotland, France and Spain, England and France and the complications of international politics began to cast shadows over Mary's gay and carefree life. The death of Mary Tudor, Queen of England, caused the French King to claim the succession for Mary Stuart and his son, but this was confounded by Henry VIII's decree that the English throne should never go to a "foreigner." Violent wrangles followed between politicians and noblemen as anxious for power for themselves as the Royal families, and things were further complicated by Henri II's death in a duel later in 1559 when the Dauphin and Mary became King and Queen of France at fifteen and sixteen years old. The physical incapacity of Francis II in a way invited further infighting and intrigue and the death a year later of her beloved mother, Mary of Guise, brought personal tragedy and grief to the young Queen of Scotland and France, causing initially almost a state of collapse but ultimately a new maturity. The King on the other hand, declined both psysically and mentally and became seriously ill with a brain affliction before he was seventeen. Mary and her mother in law, Catherine de Medici, nursed him assiduously but to no avail — Mary was left a grief stricken widow at eighteen years old.

The French throne passed to Francis' brother Charles and Mary returned to Scotland, to Holyrood, after thirteen years abroad. The contrast between the cold bleakness of Scotland after the richness and warmth of the French court must have been formidable but Mary seemed determined to put her best face on it. Bearing in mind the extremely volatile, often violent, character of the Scottish politicians and nobility, this must have been far from easy for a young, attractive but lonely girl. Also Mary was a Catholic and the hard Protestantism of the notorious John Knox and his following brought bitter divisions within both the court and the people. In the main, though, the common folk were loyal to their young Queen although she was disliked and distrusted in England as a foreigner and a Catholic.

The intrigues and counter intrigues, plots and counter plots, civil wars and international conflicts of this period of history have no place in a book of roses. Mary's marriage to Lord Darnley, a cousin with distant claims to both the Scottish and English thrones, cut short by an explosion at Kirk O'Field which killed him outright, and her later marriage to Lord Bothwell, rumoured to be the murderer of Darnley, is not a pretty story. Still later, after a bitter conflict between her followers and those of the bigotted Knox, Mary abdicated and escaped from imprisonment at Loch Leven with a young admirer, one William Douglas; this was followed by an adventurous flight to England where she hoped to enlist Queen Elizabeth's support against the Scots. However, she was imprisoned in England and finally executed at Fotheringay in 1587. None of this can identify with roses — the **Mary Queen of Scots** rose (species *pimpinelifolia* origin and date unknown) is the rose for the young Scottish Queen of the juvenile French court, later Queen-Dauphiness.

It is the rose of a child, the "almost perfect child" described by Henri II. The shrub itself, though prolific, is dainty, likewise its tiny, tiny leaves, characteristic of all the Scottish roses, springing daintily from graceful willowy stems. The rose itself is small and single, rather strangely coloured, perhaps best described as ivory shading to a rather lavender pink with reddish markings edging the petals, decorated with very pronounced anthers.

When I first saw this rose, pretty as it was, I felt disappointed that it was not pure white as I had always imagine it would be. Mary is said to have loved to wear white, in any event it would have seemed right for her. Then I wondered if time had gone on too far and tinged the little white rose with blueish red Scottish blood, stained more deeply at the edges. The little black hips too.... were they in mourning for their child Queen?

> *"While the season of flowers and the tender sprays,*
> *thick of leaves remain, I will pluck the roses from*
> *the brakes, to be offered to the memory of a child*
> *of fairest fame."*
>
> *Dafydd Ap Gwylim*

The Next

If I remove two, possibly three, small shrubs from the front garden to the back border, I can make room for three more old roses as a continuation of my collection — they become an addiction! Additionally, a clematis on the car port has died so I can indulge in another climber and one with a real Suffolk connection. Shame on me, I had never even heard of it when I started this book and even now have never seen it but I can implicitly trust its discoverer.

Although I live within a few miles of Woolverstone, as I say, I have only recently heard of the **Woolverstone Church Rose** (alias "Surpassing Beauty"), apparently a very old variety found growing in Woolverstone churchyard by Humphrey Brooke. Peter Beales who reintroduced it in 1980 describes it as a deep red to crimson, "very strongly fragrant," (important) and well worth reintroducing, so I need no further recommendation.

Humphrey Brooke, who died only a few years ago, was probably Suffolk's best known rosarian both as a character and a rose grower. He bought Lime Kiln at Claydon from his Russian father-in-law (his wife was formerly Countess Nattalie Benckendorff) and set about trying to make something of the very overgrown garden — always a keen gardener, this represented a congenial challenge. He spent two years of spare time clearing trees and brambles, then planting roses — ordinary hybrid teas which, in fact, he came to dislike intensely. They refused to grow in the chalky soil at Claydon so Brooke, on the advice of Lanning Roper, tried some of the older varieties — *rugosas*, damasks, old China roses and the rest. They all flourished and Humphrey Brooke was not only converted but became so hopelessly addicted that he turned the whole garden over to old roses creating a veritable bower of roses on an enourmous scale, all round and all over the cottage, never pruning, just letting everything run beautifully and gracefully riot. To me that garden was Paradise, imagine nearly five hundred varieties of old roses in one garden! I have only forty five (different) altogether which makes my patch seem very small fry.

I had known of Humphrey Brooke as Secretary to the Royal Academy of Arts and Deputy Keeper of the Tate Gallery before I knew of him in connection with Lime Kiln and old roses, a bringing together of two of the most important things in life — his life and mine anyway. After his retirement in 1968, he devoted most of his life to his roses, his only gardening assistance coming from local children he employed in the summer to cut off the dead heads — a mammoth task at Lime Kiln as one can well imagine. It is an interesting point that his favourite rose was **Souvenir de la Malmaison** — perhaps Lime Kiln was his own personal Malmaison, after all he had more variety even than Josephine.

Coming back to my own little plot, one of the three spaces must be for **Empress Josephine** (parentage unknown, early 19th century). I feel rather ashamed considering all we owe her for not including her in my first selection but, lovely as she is with her delicate pinky petals shaded lavender and veined with deeper pink, she has no particular smell. Disappointing. I suppose one could argue that Josephine herself would have wanted no perfume to distract from the heavy incense of the roses all around

82

Königin von Dänemark

her but it actually seems unlikely that a rose intended as a memorial, a reminder of her service to rose growers everywhere, and bearing her name, would be acceptable to her without an appropriate perfume.

Two more — what an almost impossible choice! Where they are going to be, they cannot be too tall which eliminates some of my secondary list. **Königin von Dänemark** (Qeen of Denmark), 1826, is a descendant of **Maiden's Blush** and a much warmer pink than most of the old roses, almost a coral colour and, with its perfect quartering and button eye, will make a good companion for its neighbour, **Madame Hardy.** It has the exquisite perfume of all the *albas* and I have always had a soft spot for Hamlet's mother.

Just as I omitted **Empress Josephine** from my first selection with an almost guilty feeling, perhaps I should rectify another glaring omission. Having **York and Lancaster** and the **White Rose of York,** I must settle for the **Red Rose of Lancaster,** *rosa gallica officinalis.* After all, I have already mentioned this apothecary's rose in various connections, the making of perfume, its medicinal quality and the fact that it is the oldest of the *gallicas.* It is said to have been brought to Europe by the Crusaders in the twelfth century but the likelihood is that it is much, much older, a true rose of history, perhaps pre-history. Just outside the window, I shall appreciate its legendary perfume.....

> *"She wrayeth her thorn with fayr colour and good smell. Among all the floures of the worlde the floure of the rose is cheyf and beeryth ye pryse. And by cause of vertues and sweete smelle and savour. For by fayreness they fede the syghte: and playseth the smelle by odour, the touche by softe handlynge. And wythstondeth and socouryth by vertue ayenst many syknesses and evylles."*
>
> Liber de proprietatibus rerum
> Trans. Trevisa 1495

Rosa Carina

ANNE REA, DIP.A.D., trained at Canterbury College of Art where she obtained a degree in graphic design and illustration in 1973. Since then she has combined her painting with work as a freelance designer and illustrator in a wide variety of projects notably a number of award-winning films for which she has prepared numerous animated and illustrative sequences.

In the fine art field she enjoys painting the nooks and crannies of the Suffolk landscape, old barns, hedgerows and meadows, also studies of garden and wild flowers. She works primarily in pen and wash, a medium ideally suited to her style and her subjects, and she has had a number of highly successful one woman shows.

JOSEPHINE WALPOLE who runs an Art Gallery in Suffolk is the author of four full length biographies, a book on etchings and engravings and a number of smaller booklets and magazine articles on artistic subjects. She trained privately under the late Stuart Somerville.

A keen gardener, her passion is for old fashioned roses. "Roses in a Suffolk Garden," in lighter vein than her other published work, provided a welcome therapy while recovering from a multiple back injury.

OTHER TITLES BY THE AUTHOR

ANNA Memorial biography of Anna Zinkeisen
(Published by W. R. Royal Ltd)
LEONARD SQUIRRELL R.W.S., R.E. A biographical scrapbook
LEONARD SQUIRRELL — Etchings & Engravings
THE LIFE & WORK OF MARTIN KIDNER
VERNON WARD — An Edwardian Childhood
Published by the Antique Collectors Club unless stated otherwise

Roses mentioned in this book were obtained from:

INDEX OF ROSES

SELECTED BIBLIOGRAPHY

Theo Aronson - Napoleon and Josephine *Murray* 1990

David Austin - The Heritage of the Rose *Antique Collectors' Club* 1988

Peter Beales - Classic Roses *Collins* 1985

Alan Bold - Bonnie Prince Charlie *Pitkin* 1973

Vincent Cronin - Louis XIV *Collins* 1964

John Fisher - The Companion to Roses *Viking* 1986

Edward Fitzgerald - The Rubaiyat of Omar Khayyam Trans.

H.L.V. Fletcher - The Rose Anthology *Newnes* 1963

Antonia Fraser - Mary, Queen of Scots *Weidenfeld & Nicholson* 1969

Charles Ganz - A Fitzgerald Medley 1933

Trevor Griffiths - The Book of Classic Old Roses *Michael Joseph* 1986

Jack Harkness - The Makers of Heavenly Roses *Souvenir Press* 1985

Frank Hussey - Old Fitz *Boydell* 1974

Gertrude Jekyll - Roses for English Gardens *Antique Collectors' Club* 1982

Gertrude Jekyll - A Gardener's Testament *Antique Collectors' Club* 1982

Wilhelm Kordes - Roses *Souvenir Press* 1964

Robert Bernard Martin - With Friends Possessed - a life of Edward Fitzgerald *Faber* 1984

Alfred McKinley - The life of Edward Fitzgerald *Terhune* 1947

Nancy Mitford - The Sun King *Hamish Hamilton* 1966

Jean Plaidy - Mary, Queen of Scots *Robert Hale*

J. Ramsbottom - A Book of Roses *Penguin* 1939

Antonia Ridge - The Man who Painted Roses *Faber* 1974

Hazel de Rougetel - A Heritage of Roses *Unwin Hyman* 1988

Sacheverell Sitwell - Great Palaces *Weidenfeld & Nicholson* 1974

W.M. Thackery - W.M. Thackery & Edward Fitzgerald - a literary friendship

Graham Stuart Thomas - The Complete Flower Paintings and Drawings of Graham Stuart Thomas *Thames & Hudson* 1987

Graham Stuart Thomas - A Garden of Roses *Penguin Bks/R.H.S.* 1987

Michelle Verrier - Fantin-Latour *Academy* 1987

Josephine Walpole - Anna-a Memorial Biography of Anna Zinkeisen *Royle Publications* 1978

Josephine Walpole - Here They Lived *Baron Publishing* 1986

Look at roses when oppressed by weariness or grief,
Look at roses and restore spent hope and lost belief —
In the meaning of this life and of heaven above.
Look at roses if you ever doubt that God is Love.
                                                    PATIENCE STRONG